START-UP
GEOGRAPHY

JOURNEY TO SCHOOL

Anna Lee

Evans

Published by Evans Brothers Limited
2A Portman Mansions
Chiltern Street
London W1U 6NR

© Evans Brothers Limited 2003
Reprinted 2004, 2005
Produced for Evans Brothers Limited by
White-Thomson Publishing Ltd.
2/3 St Andrew's Place
Lewes, East Sussex BN7 1UP

Printed in China by W K T Co. Ltd.

Editor: Elaine Fuoco-Lang
Consultants: Lorraine Harrison, Senior Lecturer in
Geography Education at the University of Brighton
and Christine Bentall, Key Stage One teacher at
St Bartholomew's Church of England Primary
School, Brighton.
Designer: Tessa Barwick
Map artwork: The Map Studio

Cover: All photographs by Chris Fairclough

British Library Cataloguing in Publication Data
Lee, Anna
    Journey to school. - (Start-up geography)
    1.Urban transportation - Juvenile literature 2.School
        children - transportation - Juvenile literature
    I.Title
    388.4

ISBN: 0 237 52459 7

Picture acknowledgements
All photographs by Chris Fairclough except Royal Mail
Group plc 8; Alan Towse 9.

Acknowledgements
The publishers would like to thank staff, students and
parents at Dodmire Infant School, Darlington, for their
involvement in the preparation of this book.

Contents

School and home

▼ **Our school is on Rydal Street, in a town called Darlington.**

Everyone in our class lives in Darlington, but our homes are all in different places.

school   street   town   homes

◀ **Shirley lives in a house close to school.**

▶ **Alex lives in a flat a long way away.**

Every home has a different address.

house   close   flat   address

Looking at addresses

◀ **Shirley has just received a letter from her friend in France.**

The postman delivered it to her house.

The letter has her address on it.

France   postman   delivered

▼ **The first line of the address tells us her house number and the name of her street.**

Shirley Lim
21 Falmar Road
Darlington
County Durham DH1 2CN
UK

Bretagne

The second line tells us what town Shirley lives in.

The third line tells us her county and her postcode.

What street does Shirley live in?

county   postcode

Why do we need addresses?

▼ We need addresses so that the post office knows where to deliver our post.

post office

▼ **When we travel, we put our address on our luggage.**

This means that if the luggage is lost, the person who finds it can return it to our home.

What is your address?

travel   luggage

A plan of our school

Plans help us to find our way around places that are new to us.

▶ This is a plan of our school.

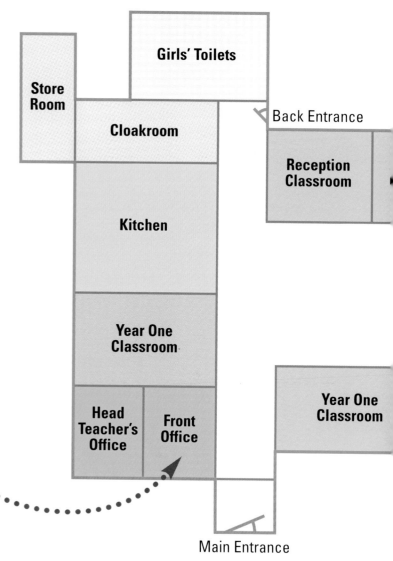

plan around

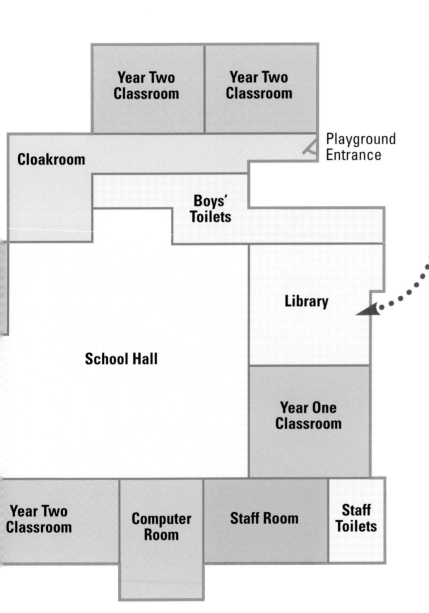

Year Two Classroom

Year Two Classroom

Playground Entrance

Cloakroom

Boys' Toilets

Library

School Hall

Year One Classroom

Year Two Classroom

Computer Room

Staff Room

Staff Toilets

Outside walls
Inside walls

Visitors to the school can look at it to help them find different rooms.

Which rooms are next to the computer room?

computer room

Our local area

Maps **help us to find our way around our local area.**

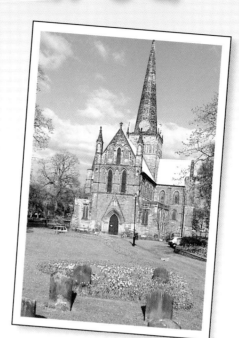

▶ **Here is a map of the area around our school. It shows some of the buildings.**

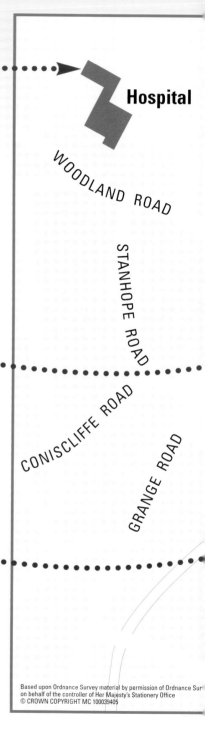

Hospital

WOODLAND ROAD

STANHOPE ROAD

CONISCLIFFE ROAD

GRANGE ROAD

Based upon Ordnance Survey material by permission of Ordnance Sur
on behalf of the controller of Her Majesty's Stationery Office
© CROWN COPYRIGHT MC 100039405

maps   local area   buildings

Roads
Railway line
River
Buildings

N
W — E
S

HIGH NORTHGATE

HAUGHTON ROAD

HUNDENS LANE

CUTHBERT WAY

Bridge

rch †

Police
Station

Railway
Station

NEASHAM ROAD

RYDAL ROAD

YARM ROAD

PARK LANE

**Our
School**

GENEVA ROAD

0   500 metres

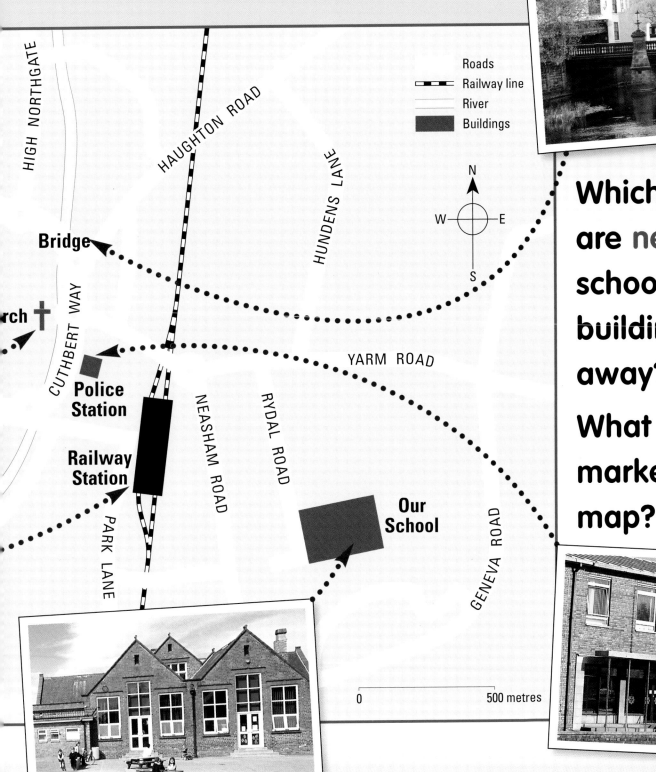

**Which buildings
are near our
school? Which
buildings are far
away?**

**What else is
marked on the
map?**

near   far

13

Going to school

▶ Our school is close to Georgina's house.

She **walks** to school with her sister and mother.

◀ Zac lives further away. He **rides** his **bike** to school with his dad.

What are they wearing for **safety**?

walks   rides   bike   safety

► **Shirley catches the bus to school with her brother, her sister and her dad.**

There are many bus stops on the bus route.

◄ **This bus stop is outside the post office.**

How do you get to school?

What buildings do you pass on your journey?

bus   route   journey

Alex's route to school

Alex lives the **furthest** from school.

▲ His grand-mother **drives** him in her car.

▶ They drive **past** the petrol station ...

▶ ... **under** the railway bridge ...

furthest   drives   past   under   left

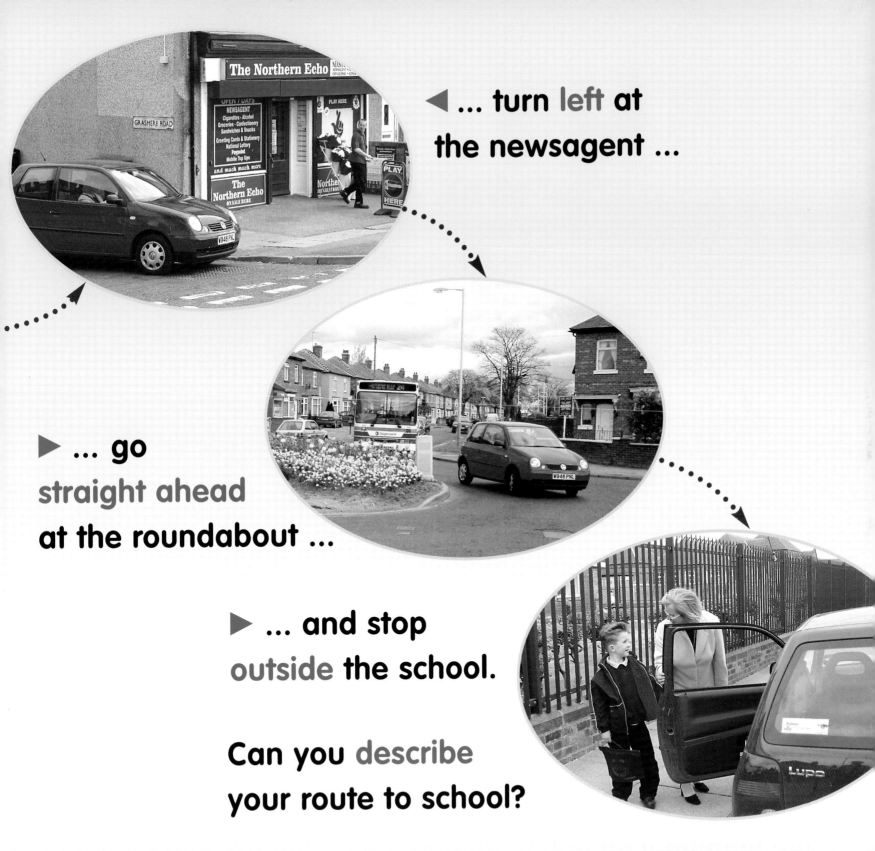

◀ ... turn left at the newsagent ...

▶ ... go straight ahead at the roundabout ...

▶ ... and stop outside the school.

Can you describe your route to school?

straight ahead   outside   describe   17

A travel pictogram

▶ Fiona drew a **pictogram** of all the different ways children in our class get to school.

▲ She typed in the information ...

▲ ... and used the mouse to draw a pictogram.

pictogram

▼ **The bottom of the pictogram shows the different ways pupils come to school.**

The number of symbols tell us how many children use each method of transport.

How many children walk to school?

How many come by bus?

Shirley's journey to school

▶ This map is similar to the one on pages 12-13. This time more places in our local area are marked on the map.

Can you describe Shirley's route to school?

What does she pass on the journey?

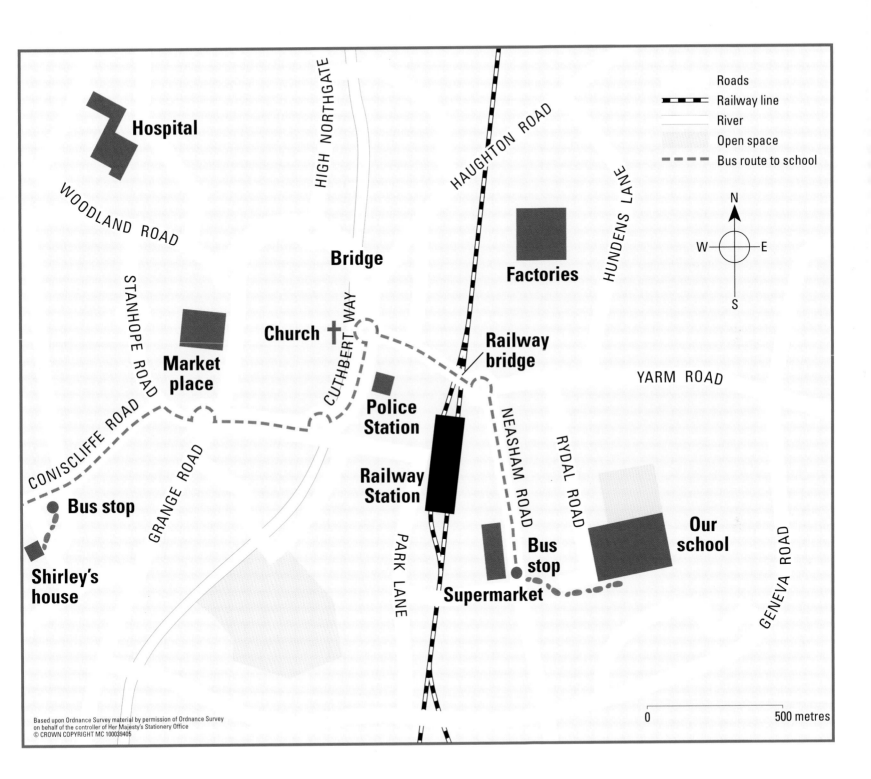

Roads
Railway line
River
Open space
Bus route to school

Hospital

WOODLAND ROAD

HIGH NORTHGATE

HAUGHTON ROAD

HUNDENS LANE

Bridge

Factories

N
W E
S

STANHOPE ROAD

Church

CUTHBERT WAY

Market place

Railway bridge

YARM ROAD

CONISCLIFFE ROAD

GRANGE ROAD

Police Station

NEASHAM ROAD

RYDAL ROAD

Bus stop

Railway Station

Our school

Shirley's house

PARK LANE

Bus stop

GENEVA ROAD

Supermarket

Based upon Ordnance Survey material by permission of Ordnance Survey
on behalf of the controller of Her Majesty's Stationery Office
© CROWN COPYRIGHT MC 100039405

0   500 metres

21
・・・・・・

Further information for

New words listed in the text:

address	county	furthest	maps	postcode	street
around	delivered	homes	near	postman	town
bike	describe	house	outside	rides	travel
buildings	drives	journey	past	route	under
bus	far	left	pictogram	safety	walks
close	flat	local area	plan	school	
computer room	France	luggage	post office	straight ahead	

Possible Activities

SPREAD ONE

Ask children to describe the location of their school and encourage them to identify some key features or favourite places near the school.

Discuss how far from school children live. Make a chart showing who lives the closest to school and who lives furthest away.

SPREAD TWO

Enter local or national letter-writing competitions.

Write to other members of the class at home or at school.

Invite a postal worker to visit the school.

Discuss why people receive letters or cards, and when; birthdays, Christmas, Hanukkah etc.

Ask children to write out their own address or use a computer to type an address label.

SPREAD THREE

Visit the local post office.

Write out address labels for imaginary travels.

Discuss other times addresses are used: on birthday invitations, on the reverse of envelopes as 'sender address' etc.

SPREAD FOUR

Cut out shapes of desks, tables, chairs and other furniture and give children an outline plan of the classroom. Ask children to place the cut-out objects on the classroom plan, or to re-design the classroom layout.

Ask children to draw a plan of the classroom, labelling tables, chairs, teacher's desks and shelves.

Create a visitors' guide for the school, with a plan and descriptions of how to get between different rooms.

Parents and Teachers

SPREAD FIVE

Show children different types of maps of their local area, such as an A-Z or large-scale Ordnance Survey.

Visit local history museums to learn about buildings in the local area.

Show children pictures of buildings in the local area and locate them on a map. Discuss which buildings are near the school and which are further away. Ask children to describe the route from one building to another.

SPREAD SIX

Talk about different ways of travelling to school and the advantages and disadvantages of different forms of transport. Discuss why some people drive to school and others use public transport.

SPREAD SEVEN

Ask children to describe their route to school to a partner.

Walk around the local area and ask children to describe a route from one place to another.

SPREAD EIGHT

Talk about other ways in which children's journey to school can be represented - charts, graphs etc.

Use graphing software to draw a graph of children's journeys to school.

SPREAD NINE

Ask children to mark their own route to school on a map of the local area.

Further Information

BOOKS

FOR CHILDREN

Schools by Sally Hewitt (Franklin Watts 2000)
Travelling About by Sally Hewitt (Franklin Watts 2000)
Where We Live by Sally Hewitt (Franklin Watts 2000)
School by Jeff Stanfield (Hodder Wayland 1999)
The Street by Jeff Stanfield (Hodder Wayland 1999)

FOR ADULTS

Handbook of Primary Geography by Roger Carter (Ed) (The Geographical Association 1998)

Also refer to local area guide books, Ordnance Survey maps and *A Safer Journey to School* (DfEE Publications)

WEBSITES

http://www.local-transport.dft.gov.uk/schooltravel/safe/index.htm
http://www.standards.dfee.gov.uk/schemes/geography
http://www.streetmap.co.uk
http://www.learn.co.uk
http://www.schoolzone.co.uk
http://www.roads.detr.gov.uk/roadsafety/index.htm
http://www.sustrans.org.uk

Index